C000252963

Kevan Manwaring is a writer ar
based in Stroud, Gloucestershire. A consultant for BBC
TV's *The Secret Life of Books*, he teaches for the Open
University. He writes for the *London Magazine* and is a
Fellow of Hawthornden, the Higher Education Academy,
and the Eccles Centre, British Library. He rides a
Triumph Legend and blogs as the Bardic Academic.

Also by Kevan Manwaring:

Poetry

Silver Branch
Lost Border

Non-fiction

Desiring Dragons
Turning the Wheel
The Way of Awen
The Bardic Chair
Lost Islands
The Bardic Handbook

Fiction

The Long Woman
Windsmith
The Well under the Sea
The Burning Path
This Fearful Tempest

The Immanent Moment

KEVAN MANWARING

AWEN
Stroud

First published in 2010 by Awen Publications
Second edition 2011

This third edition published by Awen Publications 2016
12 Belle Vue Close, Stroud GL5 1ND, England
www.awenpublications.co.uk

Copyright © 2010, 2011, 2016 Kevan Manwaring
Foreword copyright © 2010 Jay Ramsay

Front cover photograph copyright © Kevan Manwaring 2009

Kevan Manwaring has asserted his right in accordance with the
Copyright, Designs and Patents Act 1988 to be identified as the
author of this book

'Exiles' was previously published in *Green Fire*, Awen, 2004, 2006.
'Angel Autumn' was previously published in *The William Blake Birthday Book*,
Bow of Burning Gold, 2007.

ISBN 978-1-906900-41-0

With many thanks to Anthony, Gabriel, Jay and Richard – for their
poetic and professional gifts, but most of all for their friendship.

For more information about Kevan Manwaring visit:
www.kevanmanwaring.co.uk

CONTENTS

FOREWORD

Immanence is the promise or avowal of divinity in matter; a divinity that is not only transcendent but here with us; numinous, elusive but palpable. Mystics have always testified to this, for it makes a different quality of experience available to us beyond (and perhaps in spite of) intellectual theology. Poets, especially the Romantics and the Symbolists, have celebrated it for what it offers: a view of life in which events never take place just at a literal or concrete level, but are also symbolic and meaningful. As T.S. Eliot put it, 'You had the experience, but missed the meaning.' Spirit is manifesting through matter, an idea that recent science has made ever more plausible, though we've intuitively known it for centuries without the need for quantum physics, its latest champion.

We live in a world haunted by light. Everything in creation comes from light. Kevan Manwaring's poetry, which has its roots in these traditions, has always witnessed this; and in these more recent poems he explores, in different styles, different ways of bringing poetry into the present moment, the Now where life in its undiluted form appears.

Poetry's renewal is through the energy it is capable of embodying and gesturing in a fusion of language and presence; language that is not merely autonomously 'clever' (and 'literary') but is transparent to presence. This is the aesthetic Kevan is pursuing here, tracking to its source, whether through memory, intimacy, in wild sacred places or on his powerful motorbike. Awen, the flow of energy that is creative life, becomes Zen, its apprehension. Speed and slowness, mind and heart, edginess and lyricism all sing the moment in different ways across the rainbow spectrum that is the miracle of the life we all transiently have here.

And Kevan's poetry is (as he is) for life; of that you can be sure.

Jay Ramsay

The Sound of Snow

falling on snow.

A deepening silence.

The city is still.
Platforms empty.
Roads unburdened
of their incessant freight.

Trees, shuddering in the sudden wind,
exfoliate ice blossom.

There's probably a word –
in an Arctic culture accustomed to
and observant of its nuances –
for this kind of snow.
Powdered crystal
over softer layers:
a cake of ground glass
impossible to roll
into a snow torso –
like making dough
without water.

Churned up by
excited scurryings,
sledge runs,
snowman trails,
the moulds of dog noses,
bird feet runes.
Squeaking polystyrene
under boots –
like some cheap special effect.

To find a snowfield
unmarked by man —
to be the first
to place one's foot
in virgin regions.

To make one's mark
and to know it is
the original.

Not to follow
in the blurred footfalls of others,
but to be the pioneer,
breaking trail.

One foot after another
into freshly fallen flakes.
Boot soundlessly slipping
into the place waiting for it.

Walking on angel down.

No one around.
No direction —
except your own.

Nothing to listen to
except
the sound of snow
falling on snow.

Song of the North Wind

Wild North Wind

frosty breath from the broken teeth of glaciers,
breaching spume of sperm whales,
endless stillness of the taiga,
ineffable Fata Morgana of the aurora borealis.

Wild North Wind

unsentimental, austere,
you suffer no fools —
cut the wheat from the chaff,
strip bare all illusions.

Wild North Wind

your howling song sends men bosky,
makes seadogs batten down hatches —
become winter stay-at-homes, hearth-tenders, coal-biters,
nurture the fires of families, recite sagas, nurse grudges.

Wild North Wind

grey-cloaked raider, storm-herder,
all bow to your power —
mightiest of winds, bringer of the white death,
the cold kiss of eternal peace.

Wild North Wind

a grim giant striding the land,
heavy boots on rooftops, dislodging drift —

tile-clatterer, sky-strafer,
son of the midnight sun.

Wild North Wind

when will you stop your restless search for vengeance?
When will you cease your bloodfeud with summer?
When will your tundra heart thaw?

Voice of the Waterfall

White thunder
bringing messages from the mountain.
From the source I descend,
cascading into your world –
breaking through all barriers
with grace, with joy.

The fire that cannot be denied.

Pure seam of inspiration –
let it pour through you.
Do not contain it, restrain it.
It will build and build and
burst your banks.
Rage with fury
if gone unheard.

The truth that cannot hide.

The hole in my breast
lets the love out
and in.

Be the flow, my awen sings.
A portal of light in the soul's dark night.

There is so much love,
more than one alone can bear.

Share, share, share.

Give in
to the natural urge

to become one
with the ocean.

Life cannot be separate
from life,
and yet
it must be allowed
to stand in its own
power —
to be fully itself,
shining, magnificent.

A song singing
the singer.

Climbing the Mountain

Grey eyrie amongst the clouds.
Storm-browed, anvil-shouldered.
It stands there –
weathering, waiting
for us to accept
its silent challenge.
Sombre, mute, magnificent.
Magnetised with all our expectations.
Looming over the hustle and bustle,
the tittle-tattle.

White nodes of longing,
calling to us.

We spend half our lives
wanting to get there.

Half our lives trying.

And in the struggle, the
breathless slog,
when, red in the face,
puffing like a steam train,
we somehow keep going,
we are never more
fully alive.

All of our efforts of life
are in that ascent.
Some flicker of belief,
a flash of vision,
sustains us.

Yet when we get there
we find
the misty summit so crowded
there's a rota for the top –
tourists, puffins jostling on an eyot.
Passengers and pilgrims
hugger-mugger in a vertiginous teashop.
Their Holy Grail
a cup of hot chocolate,
a flushing loo,
an oggy or bun.
In the absence of a view
a plasma screen shows us where we are,
providing a pixilated vista.
Key rings, mouse mats,
postcards and taffy tat are hawked.
Thinly clad rabble
claim rubble, triumphant,
gloat on mobiles, shout:
'I'm on a mountain!'
Take photographs,
film fog.

A whistle blows; they leave –
back to the grind.

On the way up
they had passed by
the very thing they had
hoped to find.

By the Grand Canal

for Silvana

Sitting by the Grand Canal
on the steps of Stazione Venezia di Santa Lucia,
hypnotised by blue and gold ripples.
A fabulous tapestry. The warp and weft of
vaporetti, river taxis, shuttling to and fro,
disgorging snap-happy tourists in ridiculous hats.
The farting boats pass
ochre palaces, mustard, pink –
architectural confections the colour of ice cream,
a gelateria of mouth-watering delight
slowly melting into the Mare Adriatico.

A thousand accents jostle in the campo.
A city of dreams and desires,
of remembered wishes,
Here we project our happiness,
Cinema Paradiso style –
superimpose glamorous ghosts of longing –
experiencing the real
through Hollywood sunglasses.

The Bridge of Sighs is obscured
by a massive billboard
advertising designer bling.
The eyes are the windows of the sale.

Everywhere overpriced.
Would Hemingway be able to afford a drink in his own bar?
A bottle of water costs the Earth.
But the world is benign today.
The moon, a newly formed pearl,
hangs in the sky, waiting

for a daring Eros to snatch it –
a bold gondolier.

The heat of the day eases.
The earth breathes in San Marco Square.
The stones exhale their warmth,
smooth from a million feet.
Shadowy calli keep their shuttered secrets.
Carnival masks of mystery leer.
On the Isle of the Dead
poets keep their lips sealed.
Ezra Pound remains obscure.
My guide, glad to leave, nervously waits
for the ferryman of the living.

Temples and churches,
mansions and penthouses.
Months of honeymoons
anoint the honey-hued architecture.

There is no denying
romance laps
against the seaweed steps,
love sighs from every bridge
and Venus awaits in the waves –

rising as the uncertain world
sinks beneath us.

Passeggiata in Muddy Boots

An early evening walk on Bathwick Hill –
gentle slopes overlooking a genteel city.
The familiar transfigured
by a traveller returned.
Scruffily ambulating past
respectable gardens,
the dignified Georgian architecture,
that overflow with
the uxorious blossom of magnolias,
Wordsworthian daffodils,
ladies' brollies of crocuses,
budding bluebells. The sun,
a medallion of butter,
melting into evening.
The pale doubloon of the moon
rising over Smallcombe's ghosted groves.
A kestrel hovers above the hedgerows,
dancing a tarantella with the wind –
a flamenco femme fatale.

The April wind is a cold hand
shaking the grass. Biting contrast to
the swoon of an Italian afternoon.
The subtle shift of palette –
golds, ochres, dusty olive to
a rainbow of greens.
With inexplicable pride I behold
an oak tree with leaves of gilded flame.
A Union Jack untangles
its crosses in the breeze,
defiant on a flagpole –
and for the first time its colours,
its Gordian design, seem beautiful.

Is it strange to love the country you live in?
Browning's words echo in my head. Yes,
it is good to be England now that April's here.
To wake and behold my walled garden,
the hammock strung between the apple and plum,
to hear the polyphonic birdsong,
the irresistible joyousness of spring
eroding the road.

To savour it like homesick Odysseus,
the warrior returned,
war-weary senses renewed.

Every homecoming makes an Ithaca of the familiar.

Siesta on Skyros

From Agios Georgios to Magazia,
the Aegean village is asleep –
curled into the folds of the hills.
A tumble of houses, crumbling blocks of feta,
white against the dusty olive groves –
garnished with pungent sage, sparse grass,
fennel bushes, stroked in passing,
figs, ripe from the bough.

Cats lie withering, scrawny,
all eyes and claws,
in diminishing hammocks of shadow.
Small dogs pant; old men hawk;
black-bent yiayias sit on plastic thrones –
exiled monarchs, eyes moist
with lost realms,
coups and treasons,
traitorous hearts,
grandchildren and honey-gold memories.
Memories brought out like jewels –
treasures burnished with time.
Vibrant washing hangs like streaks of paint
suspended in the air.
Scooters, pickups, are parked
on improbable precipices.
Television sets are gagged –
the histrionics of the soap opera will have to wait,
the exploits of the modern pantheon paused.
Village grapevine, plugged.

Even the Gods
hold their breath,
take time out

from the eternal squabbling –
the sea respects the sky,
the wind and the mountain war not.
The earth is silent –
no tantrum tremors disturb
the monastery perched on the peak,
empty nest for black-bearded birds.
The rooster no longer mocks the sun.
Even the braying donkey bites her tongue,
mute in her daily indignation.
Brooke sleeps soundly in his forever English bed,
tended by goats.
And in the incensed shadows
of shrines, candles illumine icons to ghosts.

It is siesta,
and all good Skyrians
are as stubborn as the ass.
Business is not as usual.
The glistering shops are shuttered,
trading ceased in the marketplace.
Even the water washed down the steps
seems to slow to melting glass.

Everything settles into itself –
stops for a while trying
to be something else.

The velocity of the world
slows.
Each moment
dilates –
a knob of butter melting in a pan.
Fish, sizzling on a griddle.

The riches of night,
the hoard of dreams,
erupt into day –
as the window eyelids droop,
villas nod upon sloping shoulder,
and Skyros succumbs
to Morpheus for the masses.

Exiles

Once in Arcadia we did belong
and to its music dwelt in harmony.
Now in discord we dance to a duller song.
Forgotten, secret name of flower, tree.
Broken the first friendships of man's childhood.
Bird and egg have become a mystery.
Strangers now to the familiar wood.
Where once we wandered we have lost our way.
Mud, litter and din mark where we have trod.
Our wild cousins beware and will not play,
for heavy footfalls wait, alert to dart.
For human greed they have been made to pay.
It is from this family we chose to part,
yet can return by the paths of the heart.

On Malvern Hills

On these lettered hills I find peace.
Thick as cream the spring
sunshine pours
over the wooded wolds
cloistered from the world.

Here song waits, poised –
a bird at pray; wings worship the air,
waiting
to strike at any fecund second.
The sky is full of poetry,
the green Earth
budding with awen.

From these verdant fonts
Caractacus defended;
Masefield, Browning, Auden
drank. Elgar whistled symphonies
in the silent folds.
Frost and Thomas beheld a moonbow.
Inklings rambled, forging
a landscape of myth and language,
and Langland dreamt his rustic allegory.

From the defiant fastness of Herefordshire
to Worcestershire Beacon,
Malvern town to its tadpole tail –
something positively English
can be gleaned
about this breaching leviathan
of six-hundred-million-year-old granite,
enduring, quietly conquering
all who reach its sanctuary.

From its many wells it suckles all mouths.
Great Mother Malvern.
Her children take
shelter among her skirts,
nourished by selfless springs.

Thank the wild saints,
the spirits of place,
for this hallowed spot,
this bedrock of Albion.

Three Asian lads
on top of British Camp.
I smile. This is theirs too.

Let all hear our kingdom's song:
It is not where you are born;
it is where you belong.

Walking with Rilke

i

Walking in the ghostprints of genius –
Rilke's walk by Duino Castle
on a sun-bathed day in spring.
Following the cliff-top trail
high above the Adriatic.
Below, the white triangles of sailing boats,
the skein of wave
in a speedboat's wake.

The echoes fade the closer we get.

Epiphany slips through my fingers –
the horizon's precipice speaks
of the impossible nearness
and farness of things.

Another country
a stone's throw away.
Carsiche rocks jagged
like frozen waves.
Hawthorn blossom
fills the air
with the perfume of May.
Italian chatter.
Crunch of gravel
beneath our feet.
Cool shadows
scented with pine.

The third year here.
Both parents gone.

Angel, you hold no terror for me now.

ii

The air charged with parting.
I walk slowly, carrying my ending
with me, heavy inside –
my own death, waiting to be born.

Yet today a beer, cold,
inside me; a walker's lunch
of local cheeses, bread, fruit;
the sun warm on my skin,
feeling good – this being alive.
The week's work is done,
the year's story begun.
My love waits for me
back in England –
one of Rilke's own.
I pick up a pine cone for her.

Old soldiers patrol the footpath,
feathers in caps – past pits where rebels were cast
down. The vaults of the castle
hold chilling secrets of the Reich,
submarine phantoms on time's sonar.
But in the sun
tourists perambulate,
take their ritual libation
at Rifugio Rilke.
REM on the radio.

We drink a final cup
before the flight,

praying the volcanoes will be kind this year.

Blink, and it is over.

Angel Autumn

Once we had wings,
we knew how to fly.
How else could we have
flown to these strange shores?
Yet now, earthbound,
we are too concerned
with scratching a living
and our feathers fall
from us,
leaving limbs naked, cold.

This life is a burden
too much to bear
for creations of the air,
it seems.
What else can sustain us —
except our dreams?

Bulb

I stand by the cupboard
at the top of the stairs –
alone in the old house
the day after my mother's funeral.

I decide to start.

With the very first thing
I place in the black bin bag
– wool, smelling of you –
the light suddenly goes out.
Like the belly of the whale,
darkness
swallows me.
I gulp,
ask the shadows: 'Mum, is that you?'

The light flickers back on,
then off, fizzing –
the filament a jagged jack-o'-lantern smile.

I begin to have a conversation
with the light fitting –
a part of me
watching myself
like a shrink, taking notes.

Until
I could not go on.

At least one of me changed the bulb.

Solstice Sunset

Resisting night's gravity
I rise to the Heavens,
clay on boots,
dusk at my heels,
slipping up to the
lonely grove on the brow,
where a year ago
we planted a circle of hope.

Now I stand alone
in silent vigil.
Aurora of the day
sliding away, behind
Rodborough's bear shoulders.

It is a satisfying death –
a great actor's swansong.
A star born for this moment.
The lights fade, and, on cue,
another nova.

No desecrating ruckus
at a stone circle is needed
to mark this annual valediction – leave
the vandals to their
trilithon abuse and stoned selfies.
I have no need of the am-dram
of dodgy rituals,
the posturing of ill-cast hierophants.

My gaze is for the sun alone.
Quietly, I say goodbye.

Burning News

The old year
is an empty grate,
solstice-black and cold
as a spurned lover's heart.
Waiting to be filled with
kindling – scrunched-up news,
or the celebrity tittle-tattle
that passes for it
these days,
fat splinters of shattered tree,
glottal stops of coal,
black bile of angry mines,
the simmering earth
beneath our feet. Its fury
on slowburn. The fuse of
ancient forests sizzles.
Coal scuttle, clatter and clinker.
With the rasp of a match,
paper curls, catching flame,
spreading like hungry gossip.
Inflammatory rumours
blaze into headlines of fire,
snagging our gaze.
We try to turn away,
but too late.

We're hypnotised.

Smooring the Hearth

The clock ticks towards
its midnight tryst.
The sands of the year drain away.
Sip your anaesthetic, my friend,
reflect upon all that has gone,
the deeds un/done, the words un/said.

Bank down the fire, friend,
before going to bed.

The memories glow and fade
like the coal, slow time
locked in its fossil heart.
Each a dream, once cherished,
come morn a pail of dust
to be scattered on the dormant earth.

Bank down the fire, friend,
before going to bed.

The day a squall of rain,
the nights come as fast.
The solstice sun instructs us
to hiatus, to put down our tools,
surrender arms
as the Christmas ceasefire commences.

Bank down the fire, friend,
before going to bed.

For a while we no longer have to be anything.
Merely drop down into our being.
It's okay, we can stop buying.

We can stop pretending to be nice.
Give up that measure of success.

Bank down the fire, friend,
before going to bed.

That and what you can show off to visitors,
who guess your Mensa from your shelf.
Shallow the depths of society's
criteria. As though our lives
are no more than a lifestyle magazine,
a trending meme.

Bank down the fire, friend,
before going to bed.

The fire dies down
and what is discarded
slips through the bars
of the grate, leaving the nitty-gritty
of embers – the truth only
found in the soul's dark night,

say, on the eve of execution,
when we face the cold
naked fact
of our mortality, our swift
sparrow-flight
the length of a mead-hall.

Bank down the fire, friend,
before going to bed.

Bestowed, its borrowed grace –
thank the warmth, the glow, hope
the last star can rekindle

our wintering king
before it winks out,
vanishing with the night.

Bank down the fire, friend,
before going to bed.

The Unseen Road

i. Ignition

Summon lightning
and the thunder comes.

Kundalini r.p.m.

The dragon wakes,
flexes chrome muscles,
snorts hot breath.
A sneer on its lips,
a glint in its eyes.
A flick of its tail
and it's off.

Trace pattern on retina.
The past a ghost of dust.

A roaring blur –
nothing but wind, vibration, a visor view.
The road unravels,
is devoured.
Finding peace in motion,
fully present –
now, now, now.

Never more alive
than on the cusp of death.
A knife's edge –
riding the blade.
Into the unseen.

The road unmade
until you ride it into
existence.

ii. Ethandun

Bike black on chalk down,
leather against grass.
Watching the shadows lengthen
on this clear October day.

Paring of a paraglider
across the white horse,
frozen in concrete,
reduced to a cement works' logo.
The tall chimney billows dull thoughts.
Action Man seated
in the blue air, suspended
within his own parenthesis.

Skaters spin in the sky,
parachute puppets.

As I go to leave, I find
the sarsen marking Alfred's victory
at Ethandun – standing tall,
undefeated.

Sunlight on lichen,
a modern monolith
warm with history.
It gives me strength
to overcome
the Guthruns of life.

Dark silhouette
elongating before me,
I ride home –
the sun
legending
at my back.

iii. Racing the Dark

Riding home on New Year's Day
in the remaining light
– chasing the dusk –
after a fiery sunset,
an orange band
sandwiched against bars of deepening blue.
Trees, ink blots
stark against the winter sky.
Frozen spectres of shadow
straight out of Rackham,
a Northern European folk tale.

Absolute concentration
on the road, the line of a bend –
scanning for ice, for gravel,
the Fata Morgana of a diesel slick.
The grit spreaders are out,
leaving a chancy seasoning
on the macadam.

The cold hits you like an icy fist,
encroaching through the layers.
The outriders of frostbite
creeping up the fingertips,
inveigling themselves into toes.
Use of controls –
difficult; reactions –
sluggish. Can survive only
so long – before the
numbness wins.

Mean
while
witnessing the austere beauty
of it all.

Life, stripped to its essence,
its core truth.
Day One of a new decade,
perhaps.

The road unribbons before me,
full of possibility.

To be riding into the future
on New Year's Day –
steering my destiny.
Turning the wheel
into tomorrow.

The darker it gets
the brighter we become –
shining in the night.

We race against the dark –
Death always at our heels,
but he won't win the race
this day.

Let Not Your Heart Be Troubled

At the end of an improbably steep track
a test of nerves on two wheels, nail in tyre.
Arriving on adrenalin,
wondering if it will be possible to leave
Coleridge's caverns measureless to man.

A bottomless well
of deep, deep peace.

This is reality;
the truth behind the world.

Everything else is white noise and nonsense,
the froth of the mainstream –
enamoured by its own bubbles.

A gateway between the worlds,
here, Welsh water rises on a Somerset hillside
from an Alph-like source beneath the Severn.

Cataract of murmuring peace
soothing the pilgrim heart.
A wanderer overcome
with weariness –
asleep on a bench in a churchyard,
a figure in stone
carved on a tomb,
frozen in the repose of death.

Finally I am here –
my road of thirty nine years
has led me to this place.

To sit in this steeped vale, brimming
chalice of sunlight – sipping
from its communion wine of solar solace.

Stopped.
Arrived.

Finding a blessed release
in its stubborn obscurity –
hidden portal,
ferny cleft,
soul fontanelle.

The slow explosion of a yew tree.
Churchyard mantled in the wings of its mystery.

Numberless ghosts crowd
this humble parcel of land,
angels of place dancing
in the palm of Culbone's hand.

Joan Cooper, visionary guardian,
from her modest plot
speaks in stone tongue:
'Let not your heart be troubled.'

The Man from Porlock

He was always writing something in that bloody book –
scribbling, scribbling.

What kind of work is that for a man?

Sitting all there by himself,
looking out of his window at Ash Farm,
for hours on end, hours!
Wandering the hillside like some mooncalf,
talking to himself, repeating phrases,
exclaiming, cursing, laughing.
He should be locked up in a loony bin.
Not so long ago he would've been burnt
for witchery. These days, with the Terror,
for espionage. Writing poetry?
Sounds a bit French to me.
Not the kind of activity for an English
gentleman. Takes opium, you say?
Thought he looked the drug addict type –
all flashing eyes and floating hair.

Toothache, sure. And I'm the tooth fairy.

Have a mind to go up there,
knock on his door – remind him
there's a world out here, the real world.
We can't all sit in our ivory towers.
Some of us have to make a living, you know.
Earn our bread by the sweat of our brow –
plough, sow, reap, gather in harvest –
the fields of wheat don't turn themselves into flour.
The mill of toil. Raking muck. Honest graft.

Where's me boots? Interrupting him?

He can't be doing anything important.

Iona of the Silences

for Mary and Anthony

i. Isle of Yew

Small, quiet, unexceptional –
neither more nor less beautiful
than your neighbours –
you sit at the end of the Ross of Mull,
God's full stop,
or start.

Alpha and omega of faith,
here the Cross flowered from Druid roots.
A second flood it is said you will survive
on rocks silently enduring,
older than evolution,
silent witnesses of a world
without us.

ii. The Old Man of Iona

Bent and weathered
by his burthen of years,
but spirit unbroken –
an ancient crofter
going stoically about his business
as steadily as erosion,
taking in good grace
life's little emergencies
and windfalls of luck,
tending his flock,
his few acres,
through the seasons.

Generations have bloomed
and blown under your care.
Unflappable, a wry lilt and glint
spurning all that smacks
of the superficial, the vain.
Here, only what is real endures,
filtering through the hard rocks
of reality.

iii. Not Yet

We climb Dun I on our last day –
take three sips each from
the Well of Eternal Youth,
savouring its brackish immortality.
Two women arrive, fellow hostel guests.
'Would you like a drink?' I ask.
'I don't need to,' was the reply.

iv. Spouting Cave

Sudden exhortations of spray;
it lingers, spectral,
a ghost of moisture,
a phantom's X-ray.
Evanescent as a glimmering girl,
a white goddess always
beyond one's grasp.

Or

the snort of a barnacled kraken
slumbering fitfully amidst the
leviathan coast.

Ah.

Does it matter what shape we give it?
By the time
we have named it,
it has vanished.

v. The Paps of Jura

Mountains hover
in the haze of distance.
Beyond each range,
another.
After each slither of island
a new heaven
to tempt the intrepid on.
The end is never reached
in this life – paradise slips away,
unless it is found within.
Here, on this balmy day,
it is beneath our feet.

vi. Two Ports

Open-armed, grizzled,
carrying the musk of the world –
Fionnphort waits
to receive her,
his inviolate bride,
Iona.

Secret coves
hymened with mist,
she is membraned

in her island chasteness.
Though Vikings and monks
have ransacked her assets, pure she stands.
The emissary of the ferry
sends tributes of pilgrims, missives,
love gifts – the rhythmic traffic of the heart –
hoping her stone bosom
will bubble with heat once more.

vii. Staffa

The waves, for once,
are kind.

Cleft fastness
on the isle of staves
yields. The Cave of Melody calls
with fluted siren song.

Shags jockeying on a rock, we alight
– a boat-load of snap-
happy visitors from Iona and Mull.
Make a cormorant-line for Fingal's gaff,
pass the modern art sea sculpture
of the Herdsman
with its twisted Guggenheim columns,
bands of vivid colours
like a child's buckled plasticine.

The old man returning
for the umpteenth time
sits in the rock-cut chair
and makes a wish for continued longevity.

Into the darkness we edge
overwhelmed by its hard reality,

nervously clinging
to the slippery sides.

I stand on the lip
to take it all in.
A tourist barges past,
and for a spine-watering moment
I teeter on the brink.
The icy black waters
smack their lips.

But the Cailleach will not
claim her victim
this time.

viii. Iona of the Silences

Island of the Yew Tree,
now bereft of dryads and druids.
Iona of the thousand silences,
overflowing with subtle sounds,
of whispered secrets,
the song of wind and wave,
the subtle alphabets of the sea.

Iona of the feathered ones,
twites and starlings on the telegraph wire
like musical notation, migrant punctuation,
electrophonic chatter mingled with the world's din,
streams of avian binary,
the odd download.

Iona of the Dove
(that old fox, Crimthan),
stout abbey, a prayer in stone,

wizened hands curled together.
A congregation of coughing;
the odd spectacular sneeze
in the silent service.
A collective 'Bless you!'
Candles become a cathedral of stars
as we depart, stand in awe
beneath the star field,
imbibing the milk of heaven,
weaned on the via lactea.

Iona of the sunsets.
The full circle of the sun
slides over the horizon
into the mouth of night,
the O of Iona – a communion wafer.
By sea embraced, complete unto itself.
Symbol of wholeness, sign of peace.

iona of the sleeping kings,
iona of the sea of burnished metal,
iona of the heaven big enough for all,
iona of the saints, both above and below,
iona of the personal angel and private devil,
iona of the open heart,
iona of the ship of souls,
iona of the chapel of light,
iona of the sacred night,
iona of the toads and stoats,
iona of the black sheep and red cattle,
iona of the southerning geese,
iona of the herring gulls and hooded crows,
iona of the bogs and burns,
iona of the loch and lochans,
iona of the miracle of water,
iona of the revelations of rock,

iona of the marble and quartz,
iona of the spaciousness and timelessness,
iona of the friendships, forged, reforged,
iona of the solitude,
iona of the truth,
where i becomes one.

Iona of the absences,
we are leaving you
but within us you shall remain:
the coves awaiting discovery
with their harvest of sound,
the rocks of ages as old as the world,
stoically transcending
the floods of time.

Reflection inside a Yew Tree

for Anthony

Sitting on the bench inside
Much Marcle's axis mundi,
feeling time like a cloak around me.
Held within its dark labial folds –
cunt of death and rebirth.

Smothered by the stone tongues of the mute dead.

My friend points out the grave
of a First World War rifleman
– slain at twenty-six, 1916.
Memento mori of life's transience.
The church bells strike eight –
a Moebius loop of sound time.
The rooks caw; the wood pigeons coo,
as they must.

Tombstones nod,
ghosts slur on cider,
the locals do a Rip Van Winkle
behind the hedge.
Making a muckle
of time in a Herefordshire village graveyard.
Fifteen centuries this tree
has grown here, according to dowsers
and dendrochronologists. Counting tree rings
backwards to the Age of Arthur.
Seeded in the year of Mons Badonicus.

Waves of invaders, enslaving the land,
visitors and voyeurs flicker by –
yet still it grows, ten inches every

half-century. Thirty foot eleven
its girth at last measure. Shored up
by iron pillars – an old man by his stick.

Who, with a gleam, has the long view.
A temple of longbows, shooting invisible arrows
into the future – slower than the eye
can register, further than the mind can comprehend.
From the mouths of the dead,
the glottals of lychgates:
it speaks in silence, insisting
we slow down. Experience tree time.

The dilated dance of its branches,
its ballooning skirts of pleats.
Decorated by bright berries,
delicate filigree of needles.
Entranced by its own shadow.
Blindly, it witnesses the wheel of life –
this poet beneath its bower.
This pen upon this page
of woodpulp.

From Caxton to Kindle – it has seen
the flicker-book of history
pass by.

Moth of Flame

Evanescent as dusk,
happiness is so
rare and fleeting.
By the time we realise
it is upon us
it has gone.

Slipping through our fingers
the more we grasp at it —
as when we, in grabbing
at a falling leaf or feather,
disturb it by the
heat of the hand,
by the empty space
we push aside.

We are always moving
between light
and darkness —
yearning for one
as the other claims us.

Moths of flame,
the very thing
we desire
is in us
yet we cast it at

passing strangers,
possessions,
relationships.

Altering our colours
until we become
indistinguishable
from the background.
Absorbed
into the night.

Extinguished.

Smallcombe

The trees wring their hands,
sighing. A charcoal-sketch
of melancholy. Someone
switched on autumn today.
The shivering boughs
give up the ghost.
Leaves skirl along
the lane I walk alone.

Shadow on the Snow

Shortest day,
longest night,
black on white.

Full moon through stark branches,
a world rendered
in monochrome, an old photo.
A field of snow,
a fence, licks of black ink.
The work of a Zen minimalist.

Gravestones in a row –
silent, knowing.
An owl hoots in the gloam.
A fox skirts the edge of the trees,
pauses – sensing us across the vale –
moves when we begin to move again.

No one in sight, except us,
walking in silence to the Horns.
Negotiating the negative spaces two hearts discover
– like a sudden divergence in the woods.
Stopping by the bench where we first came –
a new couple, excited about moving in.

Now faced with the stark
reality of our choice
we try to conjure the sun in our hearts.
Where two branches stick out
of the snow like antlers,
make ceremony. Light

a candle in the dark;
say our prayers in the vast night.
Sip hot chocolate, as bittersweet
as love – savour its hot darkness
holding back the chill.
Finally letting the world be.

I walk back, by myself –
hear a feral sound in the night.
The vixen, my lover.

On Brean Down

Thawing out over a coffee,
head no longer numb
from the forty-mile blat.
Cobwebs blown.

Sun mirror on sea flat,
a great emptiness.
The tide out so far
like it's never coming back.
Light dazzling
after weeks of darkness.
Good to see
the first horizon of the year.
Scallops of waves,
striations of sand.

A triangle of tidal race
at the far point of the Mendips,
a mons Veneris of turbulence
where Dion Fortune located
her Sea Priestess temple, romanticising
an old fort defending Severn's virtue.
A lighthouse winks, knowingly.

Beyond, the ample mound of Steep Holm
and mastectomied Flat Holm.
Wales – a dark line – watches
across an estuary of difference.
A bridge of light
leading to the sky.

I spot a reward for a lost
engagement ring –

I cast about, but
it remains
unfound. Was it flung
into the wind
in a moment of rage?

As I once cast a mermaid's stone
back into the churning waves,
howling a primal cry of anguish.

Wanting the sea to shatter my headland.
Needing the heart's spring clean.

Wall in the Woods

Along a tangled way I wended
unpicking the stitching of my thoughts,
revisiting the mind's invisible divisions,
until there it stood.

Tumbledown barrier
overcome
by stumbled trees,
storm-snapped branches.
Wedges of limestone
covered in maps of lichen,
thirsty moss, panting ferns,
rusting vines of wire
grafted to the bough's skin.
A good few days' graft –
each stone an effort;
a rough-thumbed thought,
a pipe's pungent respiration.
Chosen and placed
with deliberation;
held by gravity's cement.
Demarcating
space.
Green air
the same on both sides.
A wildernessed wood
criss-crossed with rotting boughs,
a paradise of fungus.
An Eden of decay.
Gap-toothed wall,
an absence big enough to walk through.

What good does it do?

What good
these barriers
we place between us
when
in the end
we are in the woods
together?

Holeness

More holes than stone –
pockmarked and riddled
with many unspoken questions.
Ancient mysteries, ancestral wisdom.
Only the silent stone knows
what secrets have been whispered to it.

I park up, vault the gate, ensconce myself in
a peaceful field of long grass –
until an armed PC arrives promptly to check out
that my picnic isn't a terrorist activity.

Protecting a Royal's rear entrance,
doing his duty, pleasant enough,
he asks if I'm into ley lines.
Do I look like a drowsy dowser?
My pen my pendulum, I smile.
Our talk ends with Vikings
on a Manx isle.
Satisfied of my threat level, the officer
leaves me up to my eyeballs in ox-eye daisies.

Once more quietude settles
on an avenue of trees lining a lonely road
beyond the Ragged Cot.
I kneel before the Long Stone,
worn out, feeling a kinship
with its weathered surface.

A couple of days past the peak
of the year – a time to pause
at the summit of light,

before the slow descent
into the night of winter.

The effort finally stops.
The talking finally stops.
The business finally stops.
A bird sings; trees sigh.

And I pass through the holes
that solitude brings.

Sabrina Rises

Watching for the wave –
the slow anticipation, then
a prismatic flash of kingfisher.
The brown estuary flowing
like melting chocolate.

Stillness, after the race here,
rushing like the Severn's spring tide
to catch it, to cut it off at the pass.

Snaking, winding, finding the right
channels; attuning to the equinoctial energy,
feeling the quickening of spring –
nature's adrenalin – in my waters.

Sitting on the bank, unknowing –
will it make an appearance?
Have I got the time right?
Am I a spring fool?
A year on since I was last here.
Now a local – but not in the way
I expected. Life throws some curve balls.
Twists and turns in the way you
don't expect –
like a headstrong river, shouting.

Nature is in charge.
Life surges on, insisting we
free the golden child
from the walls of Gloucester.
Salmon of Llyn Llyw, swim to me.
Emancipate me from mundanity,

from the shackles of self-doubt,
the mind's jailer.

The balance between light and dark
shifts and we turn to brighter days.
Wave of spring, bring me
good fortune; rude health;
freedom to follow
my star – a surfer on the tide,
standing proud, dawn rider
on the crest of the future.

Let Love Be Our River

Let love be our river:
we have far to go –
it will carry us.

It will carry us
on its strong back
in smooth strides.

We do not have to struggle;
merely surrender
to its selfless embrace.

It has travelled far.
It is old and wise.
Within its liquid skeleton

the memory of mountains.
It has known the bitterness of oceans,
the tears of the sky.

Sometimes, it bursts its banks. Overwhelms.
Sometimes its way is blocked by sluices and weirs.
Surrender to ecstasy, the river sings.

The river knows where it is going
even if we cannot see around its bends,
its many strange windings.

It will get us there in the end.
The patient sea
awaits.

Let love be our river;
it will carry us,
it will carry us.

The Green Days

i. The Bright Ribbons of May

The bright ribbons of May
plait the pole of the World-Tree.
The children laugh on the lawn,
eyes shining with story wonder.
Young men and maidens
dance the ancient dance.
Hope whispers from the hedgerows.
The land smiles again.
The widow of winter
to her summer wardrobe turns,
as from ancient roots a spring brings
clear messages from the dark.
The seven sisters in their prettiest dresses
circle, eyes flashing,
spells in their hair,
knowing truths
unspoken on their lips.
And between two fires
the stoic herds are driven
to fairer pastures.

Hawkwood College Open Day

ii. A Green Way

The fecund earth
breathes
damp green goodness.
Plums ripe on the tongue
– plucked from the old garden –
release their slow sunlight.

Naked in the dark, glistening,
reborn from the hot, wet womb,
wearing a skin of stars.
Fireworks explode in a distant field,
fruit of light, unattainable.

I met a man looking
for a mirror in the dark.
He found love in a car park.

Baggage lugged by cart
up the rutted track –
lowering carbon footprints
and building karmic biceps.
Sun and wind and love
power things here.

Songs in the perspiring silence,
prayers swirl in the steam,
skirls of smoke. A shower in the dark.
Swimming in sleep,
we plunge into the river's dream.

The poets swim against the current,
siblings of the source
finding their own way.

Resurgence Readers' Summer Weekend

iii. In His Element

Skinny-dipping in Llyn Padarn,
washing off the dust of the road.
Shocked awake
by its cold embrace. Its

unrelenting intimacy.
After the resistance,
relief – it's not so bad after all.
The water has been warmed
by the summer sun.
I bask in its slow heat.
Boundaries, challenged, blur.
The stream flows into the lake,
becomes one.

Cae Mabon

iv. Blue World

A pod of dolphins
ride the bow wave of the Oldenburg –
lean bodies breaching sunlight,
a constellation of consolation.

From the heaven of Devil's Limekiln,
I gaze upon the sea, glittering
like a supercomputer
working out the
meaning behind all things.

Sigh of waves, rumble of boat,
song of lark, clicking of crickets.
Hidden rocks, a kingdom of goats,
seraphim of a fallen seagull,
the plaintive call of seals,
an aquamarine forest of kelp.

Peace among the waves
on this island refuge.
A sanctuary
from the world's insanity.

Sipping a pint in the sun
outside the Marisco,
savouring the stillness,
toasting the hiatus.

The view from the height of the year.

Lundy

v. Silent Circle

At Ridgeway's terminus
we searched for a crop circle
that was not there.

I, dragging my feet with scepticism.
You, on a different planet.

Drawing a blank,
we all but gave up.
Walking back,
we found a shrine
on a wooded barrow
to a young biker,
a flower, a laminated elegy,
beech trees keeping their own counsel.

We wandered
apart
through listening wheat,
deep in ourselves,
and when I turned around
you were not there.

By Silbury Hill

Lines in the Sand

composed while Writer-in-Residence, El Gouna, Egypt

i. Hermit Crabs

Feeling our heavy footfalls,
the tiny crabs on the beach
scuttle into their little bolt-holes.

Lines in the sand
washed away every night.
I hear every language
except my own.

Where is the Rosetta Stone
that will unlock
the mysteries of others?
That will decode
the inscrutable enigma
of our neighbour?

We live locked
in puffed-up paradigms –
hermit crabs,
covered in our accretion of
conceits and cynicism,
prejudices and vices,
behind which we hide.

Understanding the common tongue
of sea, sand and sun
but unable to talk
to the person next to us,
we roast on the beach,
oblivious.

ii. Desert Brother

for Jay

A continent away
(two seas and half a country),
I feel closer to you
than anyone here
in this tourist utopia
of five-star restaurants
and seven-star hotels.
Isolated amid the holiday-makers,
the diners, the din of opinion,
I read your poems from the desert
(written a month before,
across the Red Sea –
signs from Sinai)
at soul's midnight, at first light,
and hear the muezzin of my heart.
In their wise music,
their humility and humanity,
their silence and presence
I can reside at peace.

They are a sanctuary,
as when,
showing me Bedouin hospitality
in a Cotswold town,
you let me stay,
a leather-clad traveller,
in your spare room,
share your golden home.

In a few words
reduced to ones and zeroes
– the Self and the World

the i in the universe –
I know you understand.

You say,
appreciating your transparency
in the asking is the answering.
Thank you for hearing me.
To be heard with the heart
makes all the difference.

Sounds carry far in a desert
but few hear its song,
yet you,
with ears like a fennec,
listen
with all your being.

Many speak,
few say anything –
but your words are full of listening
and I hear you.

iii. Bedouin Woman

On our desert trek, at the end
of a jarring jeep-drive,
there you were.
Nomad woman wreathed
in black, flowers, the moon –
what fire flashes beneath
the veil of your faith?
In your eyes I glimpse
the heart of the desert.
Beyond the burning sands,
an oasis.

Holding your two camels,
proud, you deign
to allow me the privilege
to take your photograph.

But not your soul.

You sit there in the dust
with dignity.
The heat and the harshness are your home.
You are free of our Western weaknesses.
We are the ones
who are tethered by our lifestyles,
hobbled by our schedules,
trapped behind
our video-camera view of the world.

What is it like
inside the freedom
of your enclosure?
What is it like
being you?
Are you happy?
Do you dream of simple luxuries –
hotel toiletries, clean linen, air conditioning –
choices we take for granted?
What do you desire? Or

have you forgotten the taste of your own thirst,
so long has it been denied?
Has your well run so low –
drunk dry by your chief, father,
husband, many children?
Drained so deep that
it is easier to let go of the pail
than to pull it up.

Precious source of life
scattered with camel dung.
Yet dung is fuel
to bake your bread,
to light your vast desert nights.

It is fire –
the fire in the heart of everything.

Your eyes.

What the desert blows your way
is a gift. Curses,
blessings. Life,
inshallah.

iv. In the Lagoon

Stepping from hot sand
into the welcoming waves.
Swimming in the Red Sea,
losing your boundary,
the prison of the self.
After days inside the
catacombs of the mind,
returning to the body –
the satisfaction of
strong arm strokes,
cool water on skin,
warm breeze on your back,
dazzle of sun,
tang of brine on lips.

You reach the island,
and touch stone,

then turn,
consider your return,
make a few strokes
but half-way
you simply
stop,
allow yourself to
sink,
the sea to decide.

And finally,
in the moment
when you let go,
you discover that
you are held.

All of this time
you have been struggling.
All of this time
there has been someone
to hold you
if you let them.

You do not have to be strong
all of the time.

The wind slowly spins you,
a slow-motion windmill.
Circling cross,
you relinquish
control to its
unconditional embrace.

Above, in the clean blue sky,
the waxing moon.

Even by day
she watches over you.
A heart in amber.
Held in the warm glow of her love.

Your mind stops.
You are driftwood.
Flotsam.
Released into
total peace.
Your skin,
the ruckled surface of the lagoon.
Your hair,
palm trees in the breeze.
Your eyes,
the sun and moon.
Your soul,
a kite dancing on a string.

The wind whispers
let go.
A voice, far away,
says
I am nothing
I am nothing
Nothing
Nothing
Nothing
I am everything
I am nothing
I am everything
I am nothing
Everything
is nothing
Nothing
is Everything

Zero.
Universe.
Fool.
Circle.

Finally you snap
back into your clay vessel.
Moment of grace
gone,
you tread water.

Getting out
is harder than getting in.
You try to stand
and stagger –
sluggish-limbed, head light –
onto the unsteady shore,
a dervish who has stopped whirling.

Some part of you makes landfall,
but the rest
still floats
in the lagoon.

v . The Red and the Black

The Red Lands are the harsh lands
– cruel to all that lives
– cruel to all that loves.
The desert's dream of forest slips away.
A garden for scorpions,
a kindergarten for snakes.
Barren soil for the seed of the heart
where the closest are enemies
and sometimes strangers are friends.
The glaring sun is a tyrant

smug on the billboard of the sky,
watching us behind
blinding mirror shades.
The underclass endure
his harsh yoke, stoic in their lot.
Until comes the day they rise up –
like the Jericho rose
dormant in the dust
after decades of drought.

And the Red Lands shall be black with blood.

The Black Lands are fertile
with the silt of the Nile
deposited, like acts of love,
in the river's spate.

As when an unruly heart over-
flowing with passion must express itself –
surges and breaks through
the narrow parameters of its banks.
Amid the papyrus reeds Isis weeps
remembering her lost lord,
slain by his brother. His broken
soul – scattered across a cleft nation.
She gathers and mends, hones her own phallic power –
while the glittering current, a thousand ankhs,
shines with the promise of eternity.
And in the court of death's king
the fickle heart must measure itself
against the feather of truth.

And not be found wanting.

Every moment, a red and black land.
Every heart, a battleground.

Moon Bathing

Close the language door
and open the love window.
The moon won't use the door,
only the window.

Rumi

Peeling off,
plunging in
to the wet darkness.
Shock of cold,
cries of pain, pleasure.
Feeling alive,
feeling free.
Swimming in you
– a silver road
to your window of love.

After all the words,
there is only the sea,
your skin, the stars,
the benign moon
looking down on you
with love.

A man in blue
calls over from the shore,
telling you this
is not allowed,
that you must come back!

And so you
lie back in the waves,
let your ears fill with brine
and float.

Can they not see
you are clothed in her love
and nothing can touch you?

You do not belong
to their world.

You have broken free.

Lunatic, heretic —
you howl at the moon,
sing the name
of your beloved;
laugh at it all,
the consensus insanity,

the people who take it seriously.

There are always
voices calling from the shore
telling you to come back
to behave. To not break rules.

Why listen?

How can it be
forbidden to
swim in the sea
under the moon,
thinking of your love?

No longer will you heed those voices.

The babble fades, as
you take all the time in the world.

And when you finally emerge,
glistening,
the tourist police await.
You hold out your arms –
'Go on, arrest me!'
– but they walk away,
ashamed
of your nakedness.

They cannot see you are clothed
in her love
and nothing
can touch you
anymore.

The Moon Pool

Silently, the moon pool calls me.

I rise from restless bed,
exhausted from sleep,
slipping through my fingers
like sand.

Pull on something warm,
sandals, unable to resist
the siren in the sky.

Make my way, a somnambulist lunatic,
through the slumbering farmyard
– no perambulating fowl now
chivvying the undergrowth.

The permaculturists are tucked in their beds,
the green-fingered harvest
quietly, steadily doing its work.

Not wishing to disturb
this sacrosanct peace,
I stealthily unhook the gate
and make my way through
the dew-wet meadow,
baptising my toes
with its invisible kisses.

Past the old jalopy
growing weeds from its bonnet,
an exhaust of flowers.

Bees, at rest
in their skyscraper hives
like exhausted office workers
asleep at their desks
– as though the whole city was under
a sleeping beauty spell.

Making a bee-line to the second gate.
Over a stone threshold
tracing the silvern lattice of the stream's song –
where glass nymphs plait moonbeams,
weave love spells in the twilight of their desire.
There it waits –
in its mute amphitheatre of moonlight.

Where the wet land ends
and the solid water begins
it is hard to fathom.

The night is a bottle of ink
knocked over – draining into
the black bowl. There, a star; another.
I kneel, bathe my face.
The water is cold, soothing.
The stream's urgent message
is clearer here. Where it feeds the pool,
a deep-throated monologue – the voice
of the mountains, as solemn
and sonorous as a Welsh bard.

Where it drains away,
a quieter sound, a broken signal
that filters through to the mainstream.

Yet here, in this unheralded place,
it lingers uncorrupted –
a calm mirror of Heaven.

I retrace my steps,
follow the cow path
alongside the pool,
a dark tunnel of trees, the suck-squelch-suck
of mud and Lord-knows-what.

Then suddenly, eternally, I see it.

A pearl cast into ink,
gleaming below, as above.
Witches used to scry for lovers
in the moon's reflection
caught in a bowl –
a chalice of the earth's blood
fresh from a hidden spring.

I picture happiness
and it is nowhere
if not here and now.

A feeling of fullness
of Lammas ripeness
in this blessed place –
a secret corner of Cambria,
a little kingdom of wonder.

At this time of harvest moon
I pluck the apples of my dreams,
pray my projects come to fruition,
honour the ghosts they conjure.

Future ancestors await in the stars –
limitless mysteries,
unfathomable possibilities,
constellations of choice.

Humbly, I appeal –
like the shadow-thin cat
waiting by the humming fridge
for some milk from its chill heart.

www.awenpublications.co.uk

Also available from Awen Publications:

Soul of the Earth: the Awen anthology of eco-spiritual poetry
edited by Jay Ramsay

Beautifully crafted, yet challenging received wisdom and pushing boundaries, these are cutting-edge poems from a new generation of writers who share a love of the Earth and haven't given up on humans either. In poems as light as a butterfly and as wild as a storm you'll find vivid, contemporary voices that dare to explore a spiritual dimension to life on Earth and, in doing so, imply that a way out of our global crisis of ecological catastrophe, financial meltdown, and bankruptcy of the spirit is to look beyond the impasse of materialism. With contributions from poets in the USA, Canada, UK, Australia, and New Zealand, this anthology reaches out across the planet to embrace the challenges and blessings of being alive on the Earth in the twenty-first century.

'All real poetry seeks to "renew the face of the earth" – and so to resist the exploiting, banalization or defacing of what lies around us. I hope this collection will serve the renewal of vision we so badly need.' *Most Revd Dr Rowan Williams*

Poetry ISBN 978-1-906900-17-5 £12.00

Tidal Shift: selected poems
Mary Palmer

Knowing her end was near, Mary Palmer worked on her poems, compiling her very best and writing new ones with a feverish intensity. This is the result, published here with her full cooperation and consent. These are poems from the extreme edge and very centre of life – words of light that defy death's shadow with a startling intensity, clarity, and honesty. Containing poems from across Mary's career, selected by Jay Ramsay, *Tidal Shift* is an impressive legacy from a poet of soul and insight.

'She has the courage to confront struggles and sickness, the world's and her own. Unpious but radically spiritual, she stays faithfully questioning right to the end.' *Philip Gross*

Poetry ISBN 978-1-906900-09-0 £9.99

Glossing the Spoils
Charlotte Hussey

In a glosa, an early Renaissance poetic form, tribute is paid to another poet. Each of these 28 modern glosa works like an intricate time-travel machine, carrying the reader back to the beginnings of Western European literature. Like a glass fairy bridge, its abutments decorated with goblins, trolls, incubi, and ever spiteful dragons, these poems vault over the violent currents of some 1500 years. Anchored at one end in the deep past and at the other in the present, they explore interconnections between historical, personal, psychological, and mythic states. Plundering their opening passages from such ancient texts as *Beowulf*, *The Mabinogion*, and *The Tain*, these glosas give voice to the surreal potency of the Western European imagination.

Poetry ISBN 978-1-906900-28-1 £7.99

Iona
Mary Palmer

What do you do when you are torn apart by your 'selves'? The pilgrim poet, rebel Mordec and tweedy Aelia set sail for Iona – a thin place, an island on the edge. It's a journey between worlds, back to the roots of their culture. On the Height of Storm they relive a Viking massacre, at Port of the Coracle encounter vipers. They meet Morrighan, a bloodthirsty goddess, and Abbot Dominic with his concubine nuns. There are omens, chants, curses … During her stay Mordec learns that words can heal or destroy, and the poet writes her way out of darkness. A powerful story, celebrating a journey to wholeness, from an accomplished poet.

Poetry ISBN 978-0-9546137-8-5 £6.99 Spirit of Place Volume 1

Places of Truth: journeys into sacred wilderness
Jay Ramsay

Poet and psychotherapist Jay Ramsay has been drawn to wild places all his writing life, in search of a particular deep listening experience. 'Trwyn Meditations', a sequence set in Snowdonia, begins this 24-year odyssey. 'By the Shores of Loch Awe' takes us to the fecund wilds of Scotland. 'The Oak' celebrates an ancient tree in the heart of the Cotswolds. 'The Sacred Way' is an evocation of Pilgrim Britain. 'Culbone' records the hidden history of the smallest parish church in England in a steep North Somerset valley near where Coleridge wrote 'Kubla Khan'. The final sequences, 'The Mountain' and 'Sinai', takes us beyond, in all senses, touching the places where we find I and Self.

Poetry ISBN 978-1-906900-40-3 £12.00 Spirit of Place Volume 4

Printed in Great Britain
by Amazon

36765513R00051